Super-Easy Shape Art

by Jacquelyn Johnson Howes

SCHOLASTIC
PROFESSIONAL BOOKS

New York • Toronto • London • Auckland • Sydney
Mexico City • New Delhi • Hong Kong • Buenos Aires

Dedication

To my kindergarten teacher friend – Jean Evans,
and to my mother – Ireen Johnson.

Cover design by Norma Ortiz

Cover and interior artwork by Rusty Fletcher

Interior design by Sydney Wright

ISBN: 0-439-17886-X
Copyright © 2002 by Jacquelyn Johnson Howes
All rights reserved. Published by Scholastic Inc.
Printed in the U.S.A.

1 2 3 4 5 6 7 8 9 10   40   08 07 06 05 04 03 02

Contents

Introduction

Welcome to *Super-Easy Shape Art*, a collection of art activities especially designed to help young children learn about shapes and introduce some basic math concepts designed to complement favorite classroom themes. These easy-to-make art activities take your students on learning adventures of color, pattern, and form as they develop important skills in the areas of art and math.

Learning about math through art comes naturally to young children. It's a connection that makes their early art experiences even richer and math learning even more meaningful. It's also a powerful and practical teaching tool with tangible rewards that make learning fun. The engaging activities in this book provide hands-on opportunities for young learners to:

* Use a variety of shapes and colors to create forms and figures, such as vehicles, people, and farm animals.

* Strengthen abilities in fine-motor skills by manipulating paper and using simple tools to tear, fold, pinch, glue, draw, paint, and cut.

* Practice counting, patterning, and graphing skills.

* Increase their oral vocabulary with math words, such as circle, square, triangle, rectangle, and rhombus.

* Gain experience with key concepts about shape, including size, orientation, location, and straightness.

As you survey the classroom-centered activities in this book, you'll find the activities organized by favorite themes—transportation, home and family, animals, and farm life. Pick and choose the activities that complement your curriculum. You'll find that most of the materials your students will need to complete the projects are already in your art supply closets. And to make teaching shapes and math through art easy to do and manage, each activity includes: a summary of skills and concepts covered, a materials list, step-by-step directions, reproducible templates, center connections, extension ideas, book links, and helpful tips.

I hope you'll roll up your sleeves, lay down some newspaper on your art table, and have lots of fun making shape art in your classroom!

Teaching About Shapes

Use the art activities in this book to fit your instructional needs. Here are some practical tips to get you started:

* Most young children are familiar with some shapes, such as circle, square, triangle, and rectangle. Review the names of shapes with students. Record both the shape and its name on chart paper. When ready, introduce students to hexagons, trapezoids, rhombuses, and parallelograms.

* If your classroom is like most, you have students of varying abilities. Pair less experienced artists with more skilled ones. Those less experienced will learn that they can look to peers for support. Those more skilled will enjoy feeling knowledgeable and helpful.

* Invite children who may not have the fine-motor skills to use scissors with success to use precut shapes. Challenge more experienced children to cut their shapes from the reproducible templates provided on pages 43–48.

Enhance learning by trying one or all of the following activities with your students:

Introduce shapes with the overhead projector. This is a great way to show shape outlines to young learners, who may not have a lot of experience recognizing the shapes in the world around them. Simply transfer any of the shapes templates from pages 43–46 onto transparencies. (Most photocopiers are equipped with this function.) Then, ask students to identify the names of individual shapes as you display them on the projector. Then have fun creating shadow pictures and rearranging shape outlines into familiar figures, such as a snowman, a house, or a tree.

Connect counting skills with art through graphing. Follow up the art activities by reinforcing math learning. Have students fill out graphing forms and count how many of each shape they've used in the art activity. Then, have them color in the bar graph up to that same number. For instance, if the class is making Spin-the-Shapes Vehicles and a child made a picture of a wagon, he or she may have used two circles, two rectangles, and one parallelogram to make the wagon. He or she would need to color the number of boxes in the bar graph that reflect how many of each specific shape was used. By having your students record the number of shapes they've counted, you'll gain insight into their growing abilities of counting and identifying shapes. Be sure to paperclip completed Graphing Grids to student artwork. It will help parents see their child's progress and stimulate conversation about their artwork.

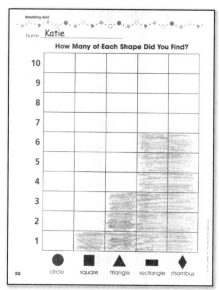

Showcase student learning. Help students show what they know by creating shape mini-books following the directions provided. The *My Shapes Book* is a terrific culminating activity after a shapes unit, or as a way of bringing bookmaking into art lessons. For younger students, consider creating the mini-books and cutting out the shapes from the template on page 48 ahead of time. Students are sure to enjoy having their very own copies of the mini-book to take home and share with families. Consider putting copies of some of the books in your library or math learning center to reinforce learning!

TIP!

When you make photo-copies of the templates on pages 43–47 consider using colored copy paper. (Just remember to remove leftover paper from the drawer when printing is completed.) If you prefer, hand feed construction paper one sheet at a time. Most photocopiers also let you place oversized paper on an external feed tray.

Assembling the Mini-Book

Make copies of the mini-book template on pages 33–34. Keep the pages face up and place the pages in your photocopier. Make one double-sided copy of the mini-book for each student. Make single-sided copies of the shape template on page 48 for each student as well.

Introduce the bookmaking process by showing your students what they'll be expected to do—from folding and matching up the pages to stapling, coloring, and gluing the shapes. Demonstrate and discuss each of the steps.

1. Cut the pages in half along the solid line.

2. Put the pages in order. Place page A face up on top of page B.

3. Fold the pages in half along the dotted line, making a little book.

4. Check to be sure that all of the pages are in sequence (1 through 8). Then, staple them together along the spine.

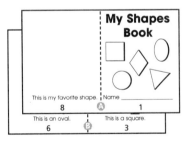

5. Once the mini-book is assembled, it's time for your students to color and cut out the shapes (from page 48) and glue the shape pictures in place, matching the labeled shapes to the rebus sentences on each page. You may find it helpful to model the matching process. Ask: *What is this a picture of? What clues do the words and picture give us?*

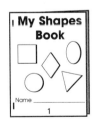

Spin-the-Shapes Vehicles

This activity will strengthen children's knowledge of shapes while building on what they know about vehicles and travel.

Math Concepts and Skills

- shape properties
- orientation

Materials

- photocopies of shapes templates (pages 43–47) on color construction paper
- markers
- brass fasteners
- scissors
- glue

Steps

Invite your class to brainstorm the names of vehicles they've seen on local roads, highways, and construction sites. Let your students know that they will be cutting and gluing shapes to create vehicles. Distribute the photocopied shape templates. Ask each of your students to:

1. Decide on the vehicle he or she would like to make, such as a car, truck, tractor, and so on.

2. Examine the shapes templates, selecting shapes that he or she can use to construct the vehicles. (For example: a circle could be a truck's tire, a square could be its window.)

3. Cut out the shapes and arrange them to create a picture.

4. Glue the vehicle's body shape in place.

5. Attach tires and other movable parts with brass fasteners.

Talk about the project with your students. What did they notice about the shape of the tires? of the steering wheel? (Their outline shape is a circle.) Then, discuss the name of the operator of each type of vehicle. Ask: *Who do we call a driver? Captain? Pilot? Astronaut? Engineer?*

Variation

Create Labels. Invite your students to label the kinds of vehicles they've created. Did anyone create a front-end loader? an airplane? a steamship? Look for unfamiliar vehicle names as you read the books in the Book Links section. Jot their names on index cards and encourage your students to place an appropriate label beside their vehicles. Encourage older students to write the vehicle names on index cards.
Additional materials: index cards

Center Connections: Math

Construct a Magnet-Board Center. Photocopy the shapes patterns from pages 43–47 onto construction paper. Cut and laminate the shapes. Apply self-adhesive magnet strips or glue a small magnet on the back of each shape. Keep the center organized by having students sort the shapes and keeping them in shape bins, or by making a pocket at the bottom of the magnet board to hold shapes. Invite your students to create the vehicles of their dreams—from helicopters to ladder trucks.

TIP!

Encourage your students to discuss the different types of vehicles they have traveled in. You may be surprised to discover how many children have traveled in an airplane. Some may even have traveled aboard hot air balloons and ocean liners!

Book Links

Bus Stops by Taro Gomi (Chronicle, 1988).

My Bike by Donna Jakob (Hyperion, 1994).

Young Orville and Wilbur Wright by Andrew Woods (Troll, 1992).

Clipper Ship by Thomas P. Lewis (HarperCollins, 1992).

Collaborative Class Train

This handy shape train is a resource your students can use all year long. Be sure to place it at child level and refer to it often.

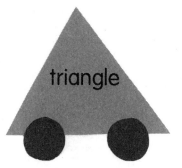

rectangle   circle   square   triangle

Math Concepts and Skills

- shape names
- ▼ shape properties

Materials

- large precut construction-paper shapes
- ▼ photocopies of the shapes templates on pages 43, 46–47
- scissors
- glue

Steps

Students should decide what body shape they would like to use to make a train car. Once they've selected their body shape, show them the photocopied shapes they will be cutting and gluing to the body they've chosen. Ask each of your students to:

1. Examine the shapes templates, selecting shapes that he or she would like to use to construct the train car. For example, circles could be wheels, a rectangle could be the rod that connects the wheels, and so on.

2. Cut out the shapes and arrange them to create a train car.

3. Glue the shapes in place.

Variation

Train Bulletin Board. Put up a bulletin board background of rolling green hills with a small amount of sky at the top. Lay a train track across the board horizontally, using lengths of brown construction paper or yarn. Make a photocopy of the train engine on page 35. Color it, cut it out, and staple it

onto the tracks. Each day, as you introduce a new shape, put another train car with this shape onto the tracks. Refer to the train often as you teach shape attributes. You may want to leave this bulletin up and add other pictures to it, such as people, vehicles, or animals.

Additional materials: brown, blue, and green construction paper; yarn

Center Connections: Math

Transportation Triangle Mini-Puzzles. Make photocopies of page 38 to help students become familiar with different types of triangles. Ask each child to color, cut, and assemble his or her own set of puzzles. Place laminated copies of the puzzles in bins at your math center.

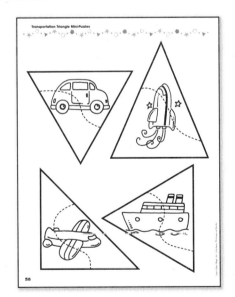

TIP!

Place some picture books about transportation and travel in the art area of your classroom. That way, they'll be readily available for students painting at the easels or working on art projects related to the transportation theme.

Book Links

Wizard McBean and His Flying Machine by Dennis Nolan (Prentice Hall, 1977).

Freight Train by Donald Crews (Scholastic, 1978).

The Little Engine That Could by Watty Piper (Grosset & Dunlap, 1978).

Stringbean's Trip to the Shining Sea by Vera B. Williams (Greenwillow, 1999).

My Mom Travels A Lot by Caroline Feller Bauer (F. Warne, 1981).

Shapes Town Bulletin Board

Celebrate your students' creativity! Showcase their
Spin-the-Shapes Vehicles on a classroom bulletin board.

Math Concepts and Skills

- shape properties
- orientation
- size
- location

Materials

- bulletin board paper
- Spin-the-Shapes Vehicles from page 8
- scissors
- stapler

Steps

Ask your students to bring in photos of themselves. (Remind students to ask parents for photos that can be used in an art project.) Cut out each child's face (and body if pictured) and tuck them into the vehicles. Invite children to help you attach their Spin-the-Shapes Vehicles to the bulletin board and to enhance the scene with shape trees and flowers. (Trees could be made with a circle canopy and rectangle trunk. Flowers could be made with a circle center, parallelogram petals, rectangle stems, and rhombus leaves.) Make sure to have pre-cut shapes available for students to use, or photocopies of shape templates that they can cut themselves.

Variation

Cityscape Bulletin Board. Tape a bulletin-board length of butcher paper to your art table. Provide your students with pieces of colored construction paper cut into square and rectangular shapes of various sizes. Instruct the children to glue the shapes along the bottom edge of the paper. After the glue dries, staple it to a bulletin board to create a cityscape/skyline. Use the cityscape as a springboard for a discussion about aspects of city living, such as riding on subways, walking on sidewalks, and using elevators and escalators.

Additional materials: colored construction paper; butcher paper

Center Connections: Math

Stop-Sign Hexagons. As you discuss transportation with your students, take the opportunity to discuss safety. Challenge your students to share what they know about wearing seatbelts, crossing streets, being a passenger, and so on. Then talk about the familiar shapes of street signs, why we use them on our roads, and what they say. Tell the children that the class is going to make three stop signs and that they should be thinking about helpful places to put them around the classroom and the school. Draw three large hexagons on pieces of red construction paper and write the word "Stop" on each. Ask small groups of students to cut out the shapes and trace over the letters of the word with black tempera paint. After they're dry, tape the signs up at the ends of busy hallways or anywhere you usually have your students stop when walking. Your line leaders will find the signs reassuring and the rest of the students will love reading the word *stop*.

TIP!

Let families know ahead of time that you plan to use their child's photograph for a class art activity. If "spare" photos are not available, a color photocopy of the picture will work nicely.

Book Links

A Rocket in My Pocket by Carl Withers (Scholastic, 1967).

I Went Walking by Sue Williams (Harcourt Brace, 1990).

Who Sank the Boat? by Pamela Allen (Coward-McCann, 1982).

Why Can't I Fly? by Rita Gelman (Scholastic, 1986).

Cut & Paste People

Families come in all shapes and sizes. This activity
invites children to think about the special people in their families.

Math Concepts and Skills

- ■ shape properties
- ▼ orientation
- ● size
- ⬠ location

Materials

- ■ photocopies of the shapes templates (pages 43–47) on construction paper
- ▼ scissors
- ● glue

Steps

As a class, discuss families. Then, ask each child individually about the makeup of his or her particular family. Be sure to keep a tally or record for each child—you'll need to refer to it later. Ask: *How many adults are in your family? How many children?* Throughout your interview with each child, be sure to be sensitive to varied definitions of family.

Introduce the activity by letting your students know that they will be cutting and gluing a variety of shapes to create family portraits. Distribute the shapes templates. Ask your students to:

1. Examine the templates and select shapes that they can use to construct their family. (For example: a circle could be a person's head, a square could be a shirt.)

2. Cut out the shapes and arrange them to create a family portrait.

3 Glue the shapes together at each point where they overlap. Lay them on a flat surface to dry.

Each picture should represent the same number of family members the child mentioned in the interview. If a child has forgotten to include someone in his or her family, invite him or her to make a shape person to complete the family.

Variation

Celebrate your classroom family! Make photocopies of the templates provided on pages 43–47 on colored construction paper. Then, either provide your students with precut shapes or ask them cut them out. Invite your students to create cut-and-paste versions of themselves by arranging and gluing the shapes in place. Attach people hand in hand along the outside frame of your classroom's doorway. That way as children enter and leave the room, they'll be cheerfully reminded that they are members of a classroom family.

Center Connections: Art

Make a photocopy of the *Family Picture Frame* (provided on page 36) for each child. Ask your students to draw a picture of their family within the frame and color the frame. Students can add glitter accents to their picture frames to make their illustrations sparkle even more. This is a great activity to do at the beginning of the school year and again at the end. Students have fun comparing their artwork and families love seeing the evolution of their child's fine-motor skills.

TIP!

Younger students may find this activity easier by gluing the shapes in place on construction paper.

Book Links

The Mommy Exchange by Amy Hest (Simon & Schuster, 1988).

Staying With Grandma by Eileen Roe (Bradbury, 1989).

Just Like Daddy by Frank Asch (Simon & Schuster, 1981).

Grandfather and I by Helen E. Buckley (Lothrop, Lee & Shephard, 1959).

Sponge-Paint Homes

Help young children learn that people live in all sorts of homes—
from mobile homes to houseboats, high-rise apartments to horse ranches.

Math Concepts and Skills

- shape properties
- orientation
- size
- location

Materials

- synthetic sponges
- scissors
- tempera paint
- paper plates
- construction paper in a variety of colors

Steps

Cut moistened sponges into a variety of shapes, such as squares, circles, rectangles, equilateral triangles, and parallelograms. Then, place several teaspoons of each color tempera paint on paper plates.

Invite your class to brainstorm the kinds of homes they've seen on television, vacations, and in their neighborhood. Let students know that they will be using paint and sponges to create home pictures. Distribute the sponges, paint, and paper. Ask each of your students to:

1. Decide on the home he or she would like to make, such as a log cabin, apartment building, and so on.

2. Examine the sponges, selecting shapes that he or she can use to construct a home. (For example: a small square could be a window, a rectangle could be a door.)

3. Press the sponge into the paint, coating its surface.

4 Press the paint-filled sponge in place to create a shape print.

5 Repeat the process to create a sponge-paint home picture.

By the time your students are done, the class will have a virtual town of buildings. Consider cutting buildings out and using them as a backdrop for a bulletin board about communities.

TIP!

Sponge painting is an engaging activity you can use to complement any theme.

Variation

Sponge-Painted Patterns. Cut construction paper into 3" x 18" strips. Explain to students that they will be following the ABAB pattern using triangles and circles. Model how to follow a pattern. Tell them your ABAB pattern is: triangle-circle-triangle-circle, and then say the pattern aloud before you press the paint-filled sponges in place. As you do so, ask: Which shape comes after the circle? Which comes after the triangle? When your students are ready, invite them to use the sponges to follow your ABAB pattern. Later, introduce additional shaped sponges, such as a rhombus or square, and let them develop their own ABAB patterns. Additional materials: construction paper strips

Book Links

Going to Grandma's by John Tarlton (Scholastic, 1987).

Grandfather's Lovesong by Reeve Lindbergh (Viking, 1993).

Citybook by Ken Kreisler & Sheeley Rotner (Orchard, 1994).

A House Is a House for Me by Mary Ann Hoberman (Scholastic, 1978)

Center Connections: Math

Block Town, USA. Tell your students that the classroom block area is a town just waiting to be built. Place a wide variety of plastic human figures and vehicles in the area. Soon your students will be applying what they know about shapes and geometric solids to build houses, apartment buildings, streets, parks, and so on.

Family-Flags Bulletin Board

Most young children have seen flags waving atop poles near their home and school.
This activity helps them think about the varied and meaningful roles flags play.

Math Concepts and Skills

- shape properties
- orientation
- size
- location

Materials

- straws
- shape templates from pages 46–47 photocopied onto colored construction paper
- construction paper cut into 5" X 8" rectangles
- scissors
- glue

Steps

Introduce the activity by letting your students know that they will be cutting and gluing shapes to create family flags. Before they begin the activity, encourage your students to think about activities their families enjoy, places they like to visit, and so on. Then, have each of your students:

1. Examine the shapes templates, selecting four or five shapes that he or she can use to construct a picture.

2. Cut out the shapes and arrange them to create a flag.

3. Glue the shapes in place.

4. Fold one of the short side edges over slightly (about the width of a thumb).

5. Glue the straw in the fold to serve as a flagpole.

Use completed flags as a decorative border for a shapes bulletin board. You might also consider using this flag-making activity as a springboard for discussions about our national flag.

Variation

Collaborative Class Flag. Build a sense of classroom community by making a class flag. Cut a white sheet or tablecloth into a rectangular shape. Draw lines to make four equal rectangles on its surface. Then divide your class into four groups of students. Explain that over the next four days they will be painting a flag in stages. Each day some children will paint. Overnight the paint will dry, getting the fabric ready for the next group of painters. The first day, have a group of children use red and yellow tempera paint to fill one rectangle (making orange). The second day, have a group use blue and yellow (making green). The third day, have a group use red and white (making pink) or blue and red (making purple). Finally, on the fourth day, invite each child in the class to sign the empty square. Encourage all students to sign their name, write initials, or make a special mark or symbol with colored markers. Attach the finished flag to a wooden dowel and hang it near a doorway or window. Additional materials: white sheet or tablecloth; tempra paint and brushes; wooden dowel

Center Connections: Art

Shape Mobiles. Photocopy the templates on page 43 onto colored construction paper. Have the students cut out the shapes and use a one-hole punch to make a hole in the top of each shape. Instruct them to tie a different length of yarn through each shape hole and attach the yarn to metal hangers. To give hangers a softer look and feel, have children wind yarn around the hanger until it is entirely covered. Balling the yarn beforehand will make working with the yarn easier for children.

TIP!

Show students the flags found in many dictionaries and all encyclopedias. Discuss the use of stripes (rectangles), circles, squares, triangles, and stars.

Book Links

Mama, Do You Love Me? by Barbara Joosse (Scholastic, 1991).

Granny Is a Darling by Kady MacDonald Denton (Simon & Schuster, 1988).

The Flag We Love by Pam Muñoz Ryan (Charlesbridge, 2000).

Red, White and Blue: The Story of the American Flag by John Herman (Penguin Putnam, 1998).

This Land Is Your Land by Woody Guthrie (Little, Brown, 1998).

Paper- Bag Puppet Pets

These puppet pets provide a fun introduction
to the craft of puppetmaking.

Math Concepts and Skills

- shape orientation
- size
- location

Materials

- standard-size brown paper lunch bags
- pre-cut shapes templates from pages 45–47
- construction paper scraps
- pipe cleaners
- googlie eyes
- scissors
- glue

Steps

Before you begin, show your students how to make the mouth of a paper-bag puppet "talk." (Put one hand inside the bag and grasp the fold, making the fold go up and down like a mouth talking.) Also show them how to determine which side should be the face of the puppet.

Explain to the class that they will glue shapes to paper bags to create puppet pets. As a group, share ideas about the kinds of animals people have as pets. Ask each of your students to:

1. Decide on the animal he or she would like to make.

2. Examine the shapes and think about which shapes can be used to construct the animal. (For example: a circle could be a cat's nose, triangles could be its ears.)

3. Arrange the shapes.

4 Glue the shapes in place on the paper bag.

Invite students to use their handmade puppets in the class puppet theatre, in the dramatic play space or in a special puppet-pet area. The children will have fun with their new pets. You might even hear a "meow!"

Variation

Animal Masks. Tell your students that they will be using paper plates and the construction-paper shapes they cut (from the photocopied templates on pages 43–45) to make masks. Using their individual facial features as a guide, measure and cut eyeholes in a paper plate for the children. Then, staple a tongue depressor or popsicle stick to the bottom of each paper plate, so children can hold their animal masks to their faces as they pretend to be animals.

Additional materials: paper plates, tongue depressors or popsicle sticks

Center Connections: Art

Tangram Sam. Invite your students to design a creature named Sam. Photocopy the tangram template on page 42 onto white construction paper. Have your students cut out the pieces and make a critter, a monster, or a pet. They can call him Sam, Pam, or any name that fits. Consider taking instant photos of their tangram creations and posting them in your math or art center for children to see and share.

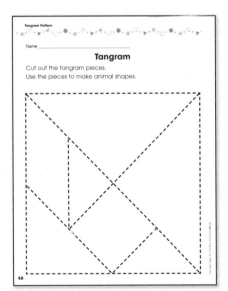

TIP!

Put puppet-making scraps, leftover from cutting, in an open box or empty water table. Place scissors nearby and encourage students to practice their cutting skills. Tell them you need them to cut the paper into teeny tiny pieces. After a few days, you'll have confetti-sized paper that's perfect for making collages and a myriad of other art projects, including more puppets!

Book Links

Seven Blind Mice by Ed Young (Philomel, 1992).

The Right Number of Elephants by Jeff Shephard (Scholastic, 1990).

Bat Jamboree by Kathi Appelt (Scholastic, 1996).

Seven Little Rabbits by John Becker (Scholastic, 1973).

The Tangram Magician by Lisa Campbell Ernst and Lee Ernst (Harry N. Abrams, 1990)

Mr. Shapes Bear

Making this friendly bear is a fun way to help children see that shapes, no matter their orientation, remain the same shape . . . that rectangles will always be rectangles.

Math Concepts and Skills

■ shape properties
▼ orientation
● size
⬠ location

Materials

■ photocopies of the shapes template from page 47

▼ photocopies of the bear pattern from page 37

● scissors

⬠ markers

Steps

Show the children the bear outline. Ask: What shapes do you see? Talk about the parts of a bear. For example, discuss his rectangle legs, rhombus (diamond) arms, hexagon body, and so on. Your discussion should also illustrate that a shape is the same shape regardless of its orientation; a rhombus is still a rhombus whether it is placed vertically or horizontally or faces left or right. Then, tell your students that they will be cutting and gluing shapes onto the outline to make a bear. Ask each of your students to:

1. Examine the shapes and think about where each shape will go on the bear pattern.

2. Cut out the shapes.

3. Match the cut-out shapes to the shapes on the pattern.

4. Glue the shapes in place.

5 Draw a face and other details on the Mr. Shapes Bear.

Variation

Mr. Movable Bear.
Instead of gluing the
shapes in place, have
older children use the bear
outline as guide. After
they've put the shapes in
place, ask them to make
holes with a one-hole
punch and connect the
shapes with a brass
fastener. (Each bear
requires nine fasteners.)
Younger children may
need assistance using
the one-hole punch.
Additional materials: one-
hole punch, brass fasteners

Center Connections: Art

Single-Shape Collages. Select a particular shape on
which you want your students to focus, and photocopy
the corresponding template from pages 44–45 on
construction paper. Ask your students to cut out the
shapes and create a collage by gluing them onto a piece of
construction paper, bulletin-board paper, or wide-width
aluminum foil. Display their artwork around the classroom. Take the project a step further by counting and
graphing all the shapes in a particular color. For example,
if you made a circle collage there may eight yellow circles,
six red, nine blue, and so on or,. try graphing by size:
Glue black examples of each size to the bottom of a bar
graph, then count the circles of the same size on the collage and record the number on the graph

TIP!

Put a few one-hole
punches in with your
supply of scissors and let
your students be creative.
Children really enjoy the
challenge of squeezing
a one-hole punch and
using it to adorn their
artwork with holes.

Book Links

Little Bear by Diane
Namm (Children's Press,
1990).

*Where Is the Bear at
School?* by Bonnie Nims
(Whitman, 1989).

Alphabears by Kathleen
Hague (Henry Holt &
Company, 1999).

Ten Black Dots by Donald
Crews (Scholastic, 1968).

It's the Bear by Jez
Alborough (Candlewick
Press, 1996).

Friendly-Fish Bulletin Board

Creating this sparkly fish is
a fun way to teach the circle shape.

Math Concepts and Skills

■ shape properties
▼ orientation
⬠ location

Materials

■ 100 approximately pre-cut construction paper circles about 3" in diameter, in a variety of colors

▼ blue bulletin board paper

● lavender bulletin board paper

⬠ glitter in salt shakers

■ paper plates

▼ several sheets of green tissue paper

● glue

⬠ paint brushes

Steps

Cover your bulletin board in blue paper. Cut an outline of a fish out of the lavender-colored paper. Its length should be nearly as wide as your bulletin board. Lay the fish on an art table, where students can work, reaching across it easily as they glue on scales.

Explain to your students that they will each be decorating fish scales for the giant fish which will be displayed on the bulletin board. Ask each of your students to:

1. Use the brushes to put glue along the outside edges of the circle.

2. Hold each scale over the paper plate and shake glitter onto its surface.

3. Lay the scales so they slightly overlap each other and glue in place. The entire surface of the fish needs to be covered in scales.

After the scales have dried, add an eye and a fin. Staple the completed fish to the blue bulletin-board background and attach tufts of green tissue paper below and beside the fish to give the effect of seaweed. Finally, make a sign for the bulletin board that says something like: "Sea What We Made with Circles!" For added fun, have students count how many circles they used to cover the fish.

Variation

School-of-Fish Bulletin Board. Cover your bulletin board in blue paper, but this time have each child in the class create his or her own fish. Give students pre-cut ovals in a variety of colors. These will be the bodies of the fish. Instruct students to use triangle shapes for the fins and tails and supply them with googlie eyes and some glue. After the fish are dry, staple them to the bulletin-board background. To make it resemble a school of fish, place the fish so they're all facing the same direction. Then make and attach a title banner that reads something like "We Love Our School!"

Center Connections: Math

Zoo Animal Mini-Puzzles. Make photocopies of the mini-puzzles provided on page 39 to help students become familiar with rectangles. Ask each child to color, cut, and assemble his or her own set of puzzles. Tuck laminated copies of the puzzles in bins at a math center for your students to use.

TIP!

You can also add green crepe-paper streamers and cellophane for seaweed on the fish bulletin board. Both materials sway and shimmer with air currents, making the fish appear to swim.

Book Links

One Gorilla by Atsuko Morozumi (Farrar, Straus & Giroux, 1990).

The Day Jimmy's Boa Ate the Wash by Trinka Hakes Noble (Troll, 1999).

Rainbow Fish by Marcus Pfister (North-South Books, Inc., 1992).

The Extinct Alphabet Book by Jerry Pallotta (Charlesbridge, 1993).

Barnyard Mini-Puzzles

These barnyard buddies will help children learn their
shapes and develop puzzle-making skills.

Math Concepts and Skills

■ shape properties
▼ orientation

Materials

■ photocopies of mini-puzzle templates from pages 40–41
▼ scissors
● crayons
⬠ envelopes

Steps

Provide each child with the templates of the Barnyard Mini-Puzzles. Explain to the children that they will be making shape puzzles. Ask each of your students to:

1 Color the pictures.

2 Cut out the pictures, following the dark line that outlines each illustration.

3 Cut along the light-dotted lines that divide the illustration into two puzzle pieces.

4 Put their initials on the back of each puzzle. (This will help them keep track of which puzzles are theirs at clean-up time.)

After your students have had several minutes to assemble their very own puzzles, ask them to place their puzzles in an

envelope. Suggest to the children that they bring home their puzzles to share with family and friends.

Variation

Document students' developing puzzle-making skills by having students glue a few completed puzzles in place on squares of colored construction paper. After the pages are dry, tuck them in student portfolios.

Center Connections: Math

Block Sorting. Encourage your students to use their block area as a math-learning area. It's a great spot for children to explore objects as three-dimensional solids with shape outlines through sorting and classifying. Trace the outline of several of the blocks in your block area on large index cards. Tape the cards onto the front of plastic bins or buckets. Model the sorting process by selecting a block and comparing it to the outline shapes on the bins. Place it in the bin that matches its outline. Then invite your students to sort the blocks by examining their outlines. When they're ready, challenge your students to trace additional blocks, then sort and classify them.

TIP!

Make some puzzles for classroom use. Color and laminate them for durability. Store them in a folder or bin in your math center, where your students can practice matching the puzzle pieces and making shapes.

Book Links

The Farmer in the Dell by Louise Egan (Whitman, 1987).

Rockabye Farm by Diane Hamm (Half Moon/Simon & Schuster, 1992).

Farm Noises by Jane Miller (Simon & Schuster, 1989).

When the Rooster Crowed by Patricia Lillie (Greenwillow, 1991).

Midnight Farm by Carly Simon (Scholastic, 1998).

Tissue-Paper Farm

Brightly colored tissue paper makes these three dimensional farming landscapes especially delightful to look at and learn with.

Math Concepts and Skills

- ◼ shape properties
- ▼ orientation
- ● size
- ⬠ location

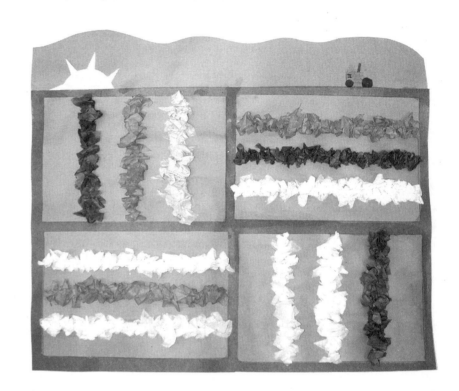

Materials

- ◼ several sheets of green construction paper, cut into 4" x 6" rectangles
- ▼ colored tissue paper cut into 1" squares, or tissue paper scraps
- ● glue

Steps

In advance of the activity, draw three parallel lines on the green rectangles. Draw the lines vertically on half the rectangles and horizontally on the others.

Explain to the children that they will be using their fingers to tear and pinch tissue paper to make rows of plants. Ask each of your students to:

1. Tear small pieces of tissue and pinch them into little puffs.

2. Glue the shapes along the lines drawn on the squares of construction paper until each of the lines is entirely covered with tissue-paper puffs.

Variation

Collaborative Class Bulletin Board Arrange the students' work on a bulletin board so they alternate horizontally and vertically to create a patchwork of fields. If you find your bulletin board has an extra space or two, make a square of your own to add to it. When the bulletin board is complete, make a title for it, such as "Our Class Farm".

Center Connections: Math

Seeing Shapes In your discussion about farm life, talk about the outline shapes of farmhouses, silos, barns, and so on. Ask: *How is a farmhouse's outline similar to a shoebox's? What other things does its outline remind you of?* Record students' responses on chart paper in words or pictures. For example, if a child suggests a farmhouse has the same outline as a book, you might draw a book to record his or her suggestion.

★·★·★·★·★·★

TIP!

★·★·★·★·★·★·★·★·★

Take a virtual field trip to a farm by reading aloud a farm picture book to your students. Invite your students to make observations about the farm's landscape. Ask: *Is the farmer growing something? What clues do we have?*

Book Links

Old MacDonald Had a Farm by Tracey Pearson (Dutton, 1984).

A Farmer's Dozen by Sandra Russell (Harper, 1992).

This Is the Farmer by Nancy Tafuri (Greenwillow, 1994).

I'm a Jolly Farmer by Julie Lacome (Candlewick, 1994).

Wrapping-Paper Quilt Bulletin Board

Invite each child to make one quilt square for a classroom bulletin board
that will help show what they know about shapes.

Math Concepts and Skills

- shape properties
- ▼ orientation
- ● size
- ⬠ location

Materials

- ◼ several sheets of construction paper, cut into 6" x 6" squares
- ▼ several patterns of wrapping paper, cut into 6" x 6" squares
- ● precut shape templates from pages 43 and 47
- ⬠ scissors
- ◼ glue

Steps

Introduce the activity by letting your students know that they will be cutting and gluing shapes to create farm pictures for a patchwork quilt. Ask each of your students to:

1. Decide what farm picture he or she would like to make: a farm animal, barn, house, tractor, etc.

2. Examine the shapes templates and select shapes that can be used to construct the picture. (For example: a square could be the base of a barn, a triangle could be its roof.)

3. Choose wrapping paper on which to trace the different shapes.

4. Cut out the shapes and arrange them to create the farm picture.

5. Glue the shapes in place on a square of construction paper.

Arrange the individual quilt squares side by side on a bulletin board. If there are extra spaces, make a square of your own to add to the quilt. You can also use the wrapping paper cut-out technique to make a sign for the bulletin board. When the bulletin board is complete, invite your students to talk about the project and what they learned about creating pictures with shapes.

Variation

Make a Cloth Quilt! Have students arrange the shapes they've selected for their farm picture on a 7" x 7" square of broadcloth. Ask them to trace the shapes of their picture with a pencil. (Younger students may need assistance holding the cloth as they trace.) When the shapes have been traced, students can begin painting them. Squeeze the contents of several puff paint bottles into watercolor paint trays and distribute brushes to your students. Thin stiff brushes work best for this activity. Once the quilt squares have dried, let students sew the squares together with yarn and kid-friendly needlepoint needles. (You can also use a sewing machine to sew batting and a quilt backing into place.) Hang the quilt over a wooden dowel, somewhere where everyone in the class can enjoy it.

Additional materials: broadcloth squares; pencils; puff paints, paint trays and brushes; yarn and needlepoint needles; dowel

Center Connections: Math

Pattern-Block Photo Quilt. Use the pattern blocks in your math center to make a photo quilt! Begin by letting your students know that they'll be using their imaginations to create pattern-block pictures of farm animals, tractors, and so on. Make sure your math center has plenty of 6" x 6" squares of black construction paper on which students can arrange their pattern-block creations. Explain that you'll be photographing their pictures to record their work for a collaborative class quilt.

After students have created their pattern-block designs, take a photograph of each one. Attach each photo to a 6" x 6" square of wrapping paper, then arrange the wrapping-paper squares side by side on a bulletin board for a quilt-like effect.

TIP!

For younger students, photocopy the shape templates directly onto colored construction paper. Pre-cut the shapes and distribute them. Have students arrange the shapes into farm pictures, then glue their pictures onto 6" x 6" squares of wrapping paper. Arrange the individual squares side by side on a bulletin board to create a quilt.

Book Links

The Boy and the Quilt by Shirley Kurtz (Goodbooks, 1991).

The Patchwork Quilt by Valerie Flournoy (Dutton, 1985).

Sweet Clara and the Freedom Quilt by Deborah Hopkinson (Random House, 1995).

There's a Square: A Book About Shapes by Mary Serfozo (Scholastic, 1996).

The Greedy Triangle by Marilyn Burns (Scholastic, 1994).

Name _____

How Many of Each Shape Did You Find?

10					
9					
8					
7					
6					
5					
4					
3					
2					
1					

circle   square   triangle   rectangle   rhombus

Super-Easy Shape Art Scholastic Professional Books

This is my favorite shape.

8

Super-Easy Shape Art Scholastic Professional Books *page 33*

My Shapes Book

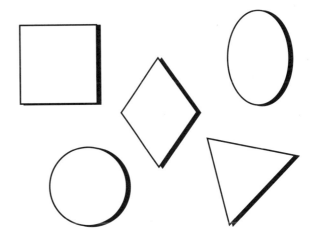

Name _____

1

Ⓐ

Ⓑ

This is an oval.

6

This is a square.

3

⚫

This is a circle.

2

◆

This is a rhombus.

7

▲

This is a triangle.

4

▬

This is a rectangle.

5

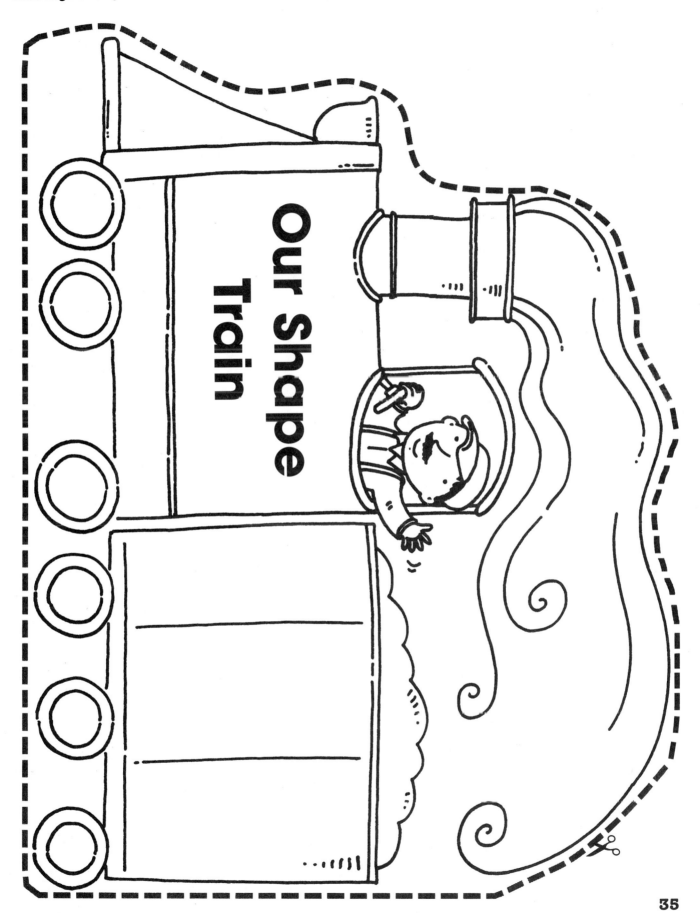

Our Shape Train

My Family

Super-Easy Shape Art Scholastic Professional Books

Name _____

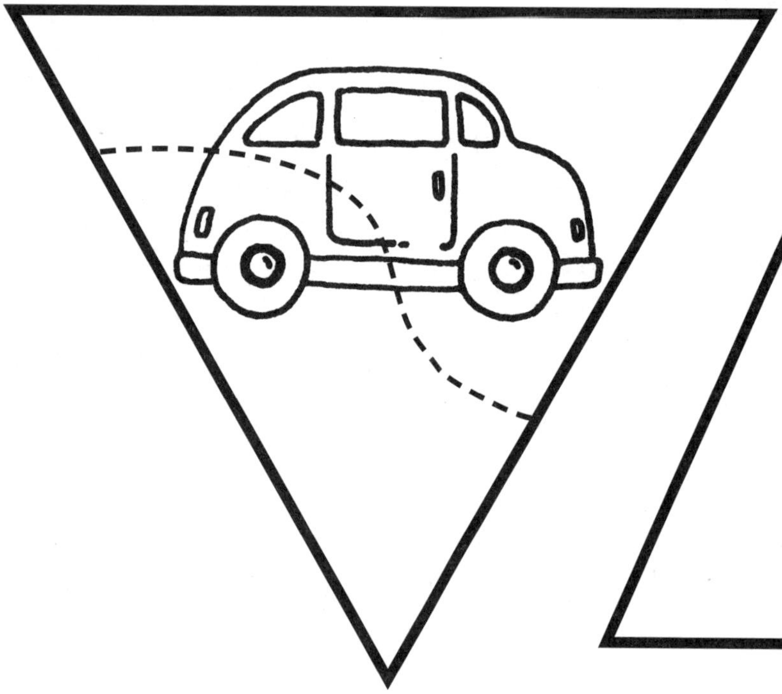

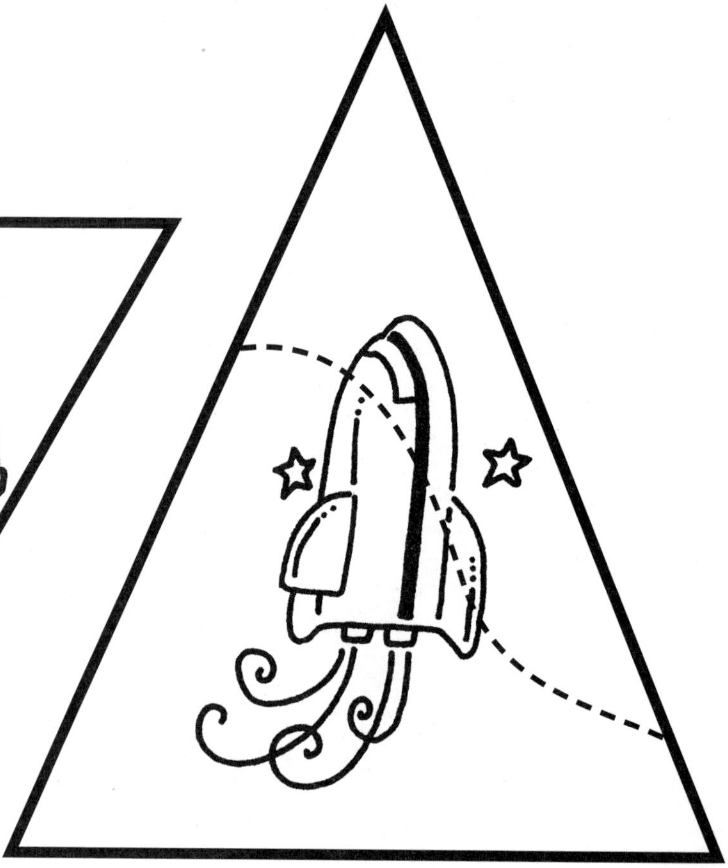

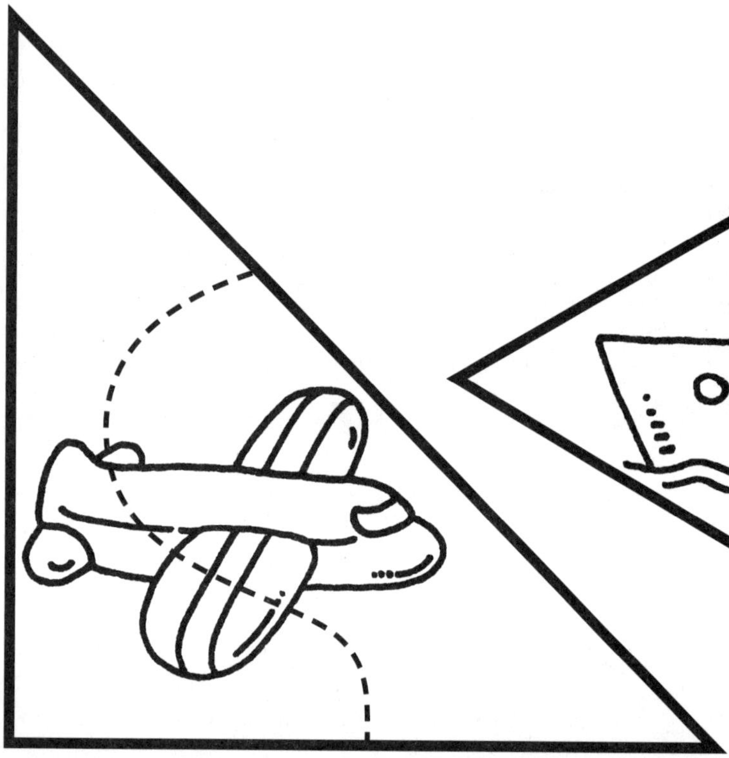

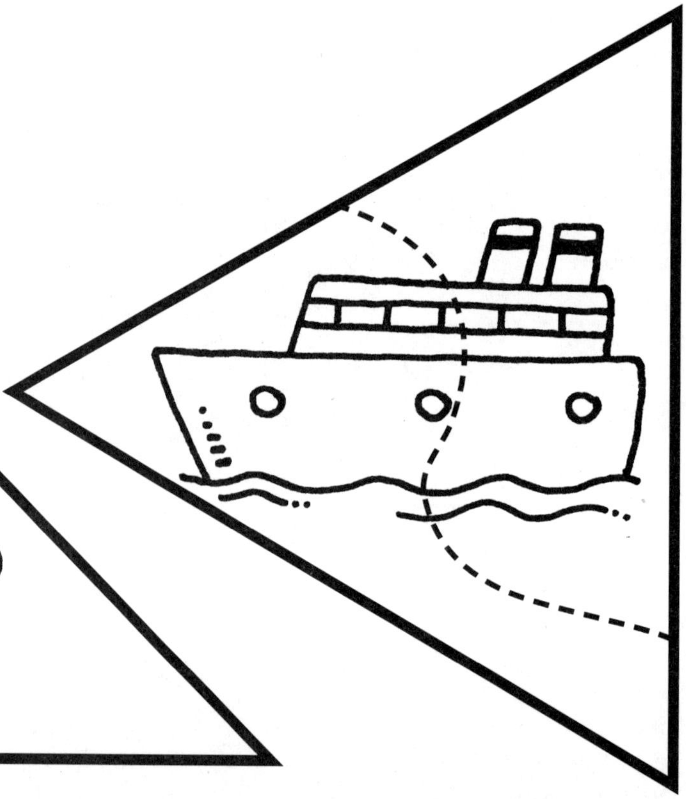

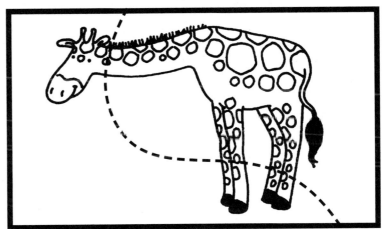

39

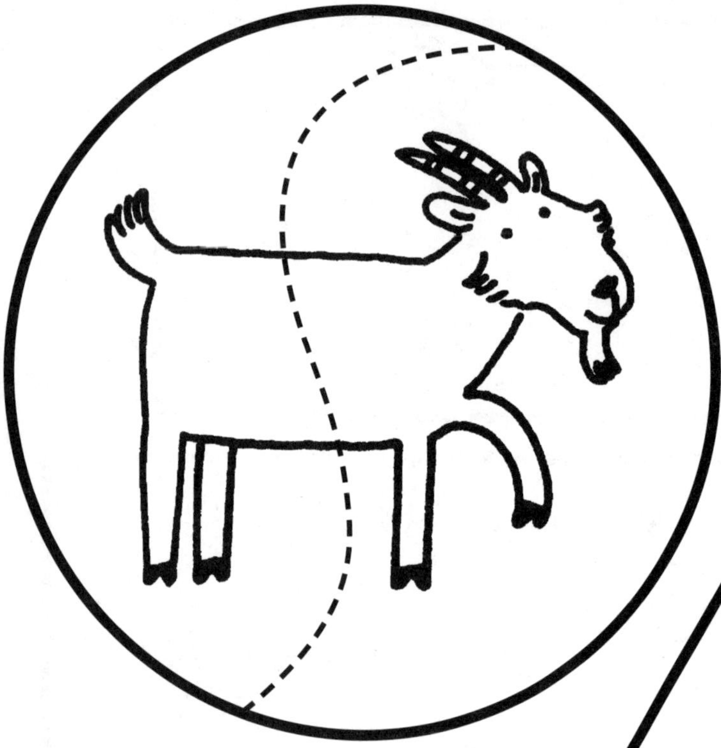

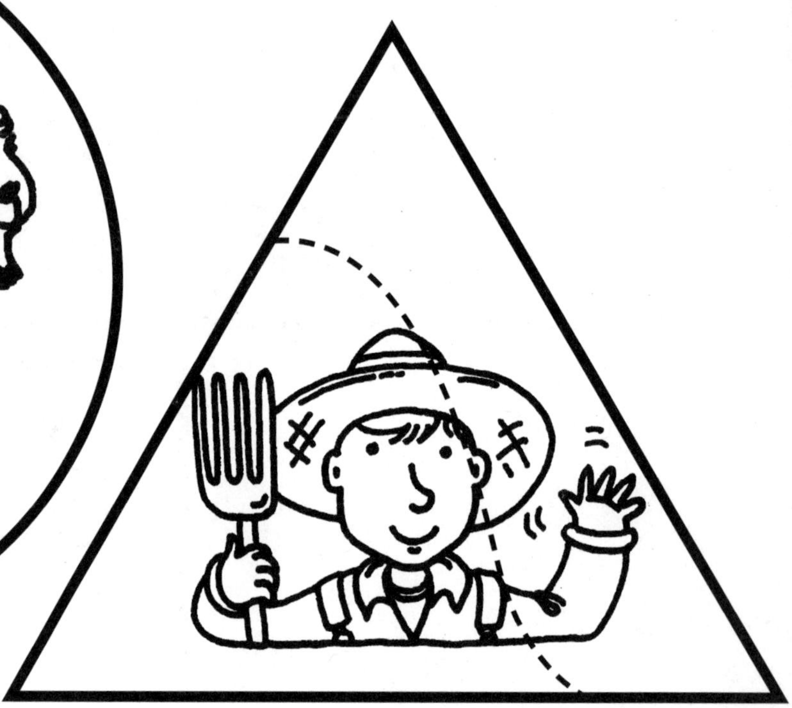

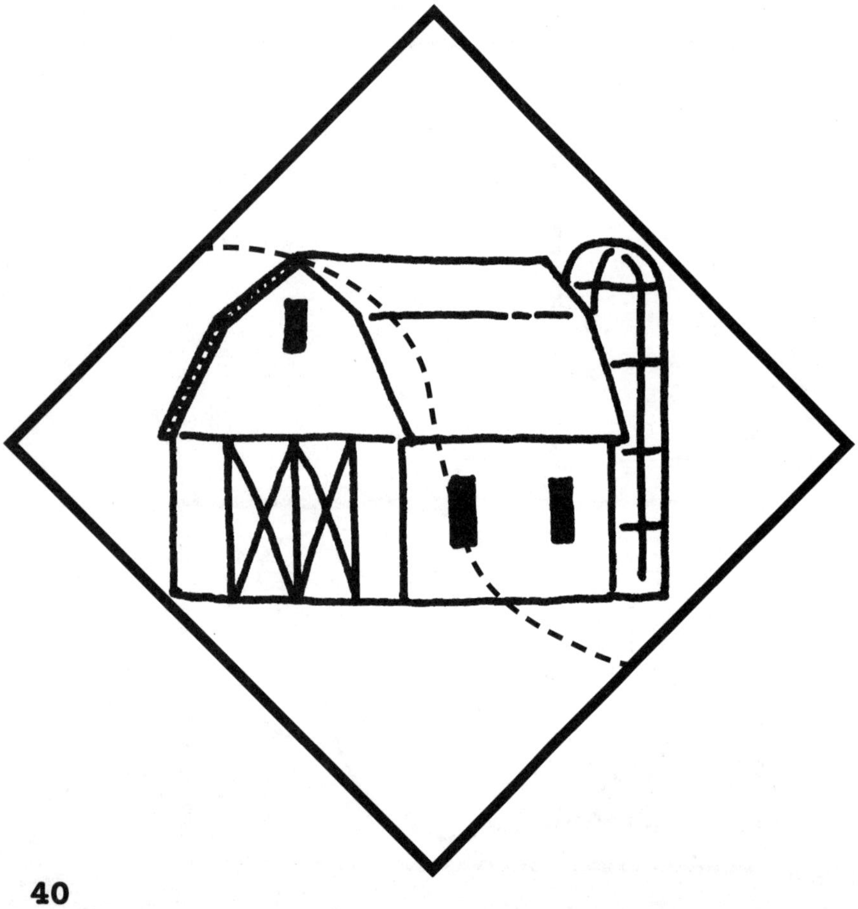

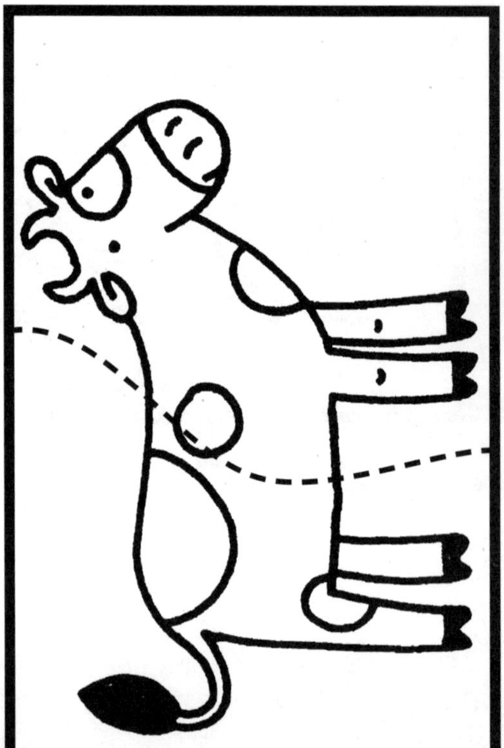

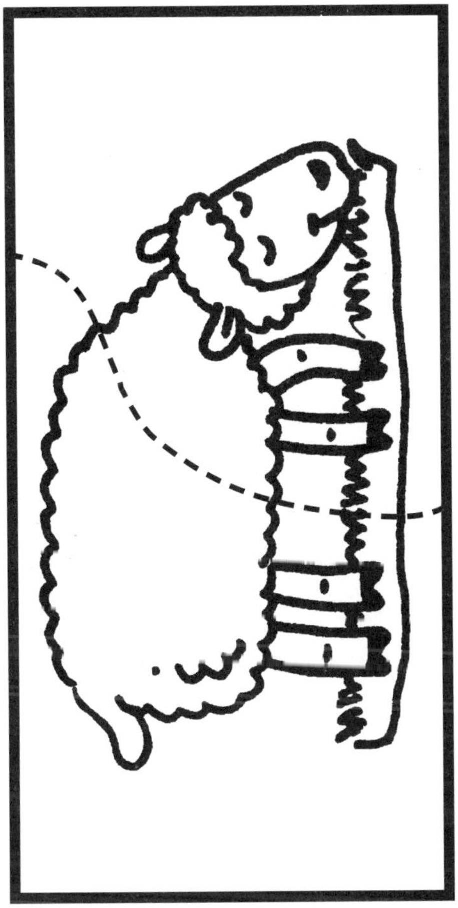

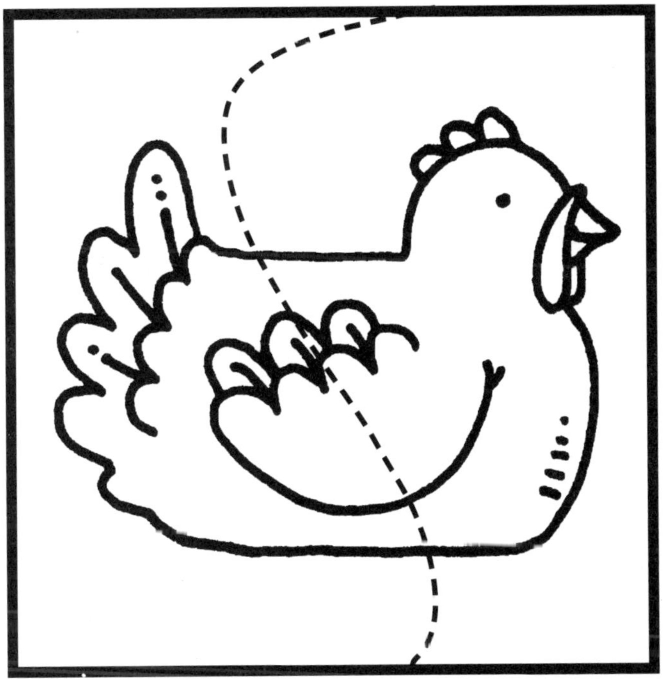

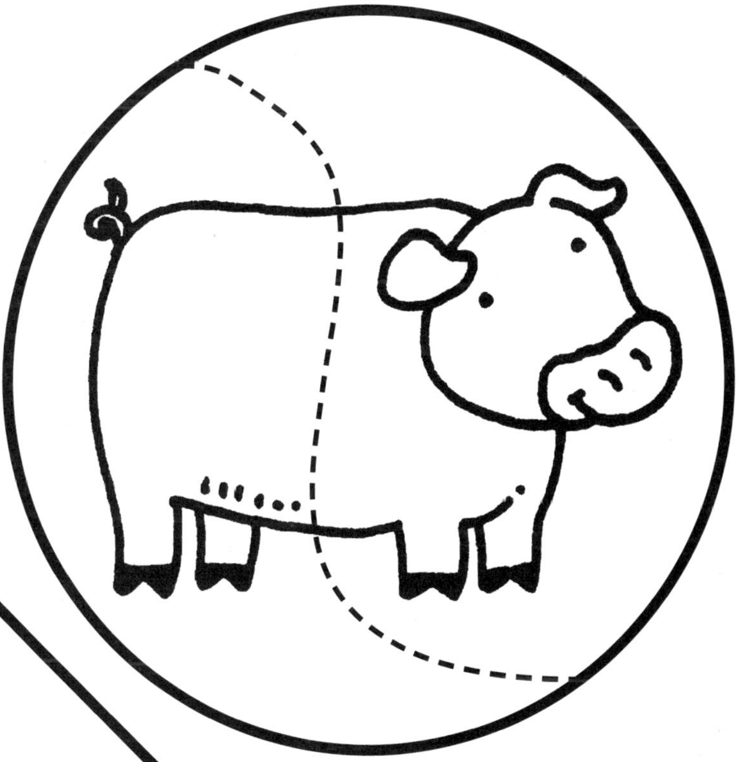

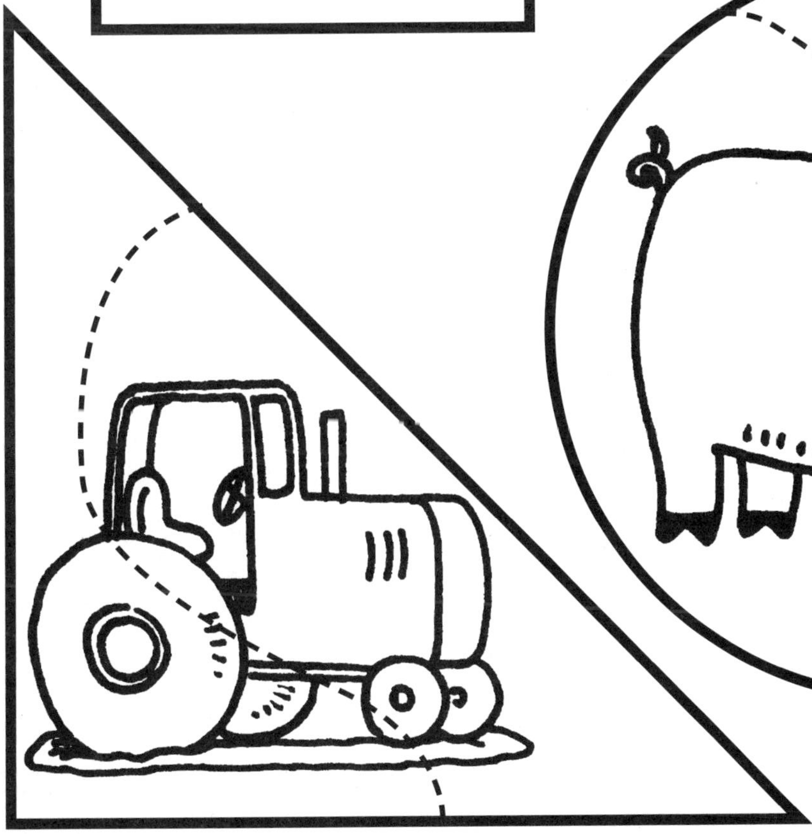

Name _____

Tangram

Cut out the tangram pieces.

Use the pieces to make animal shapes.

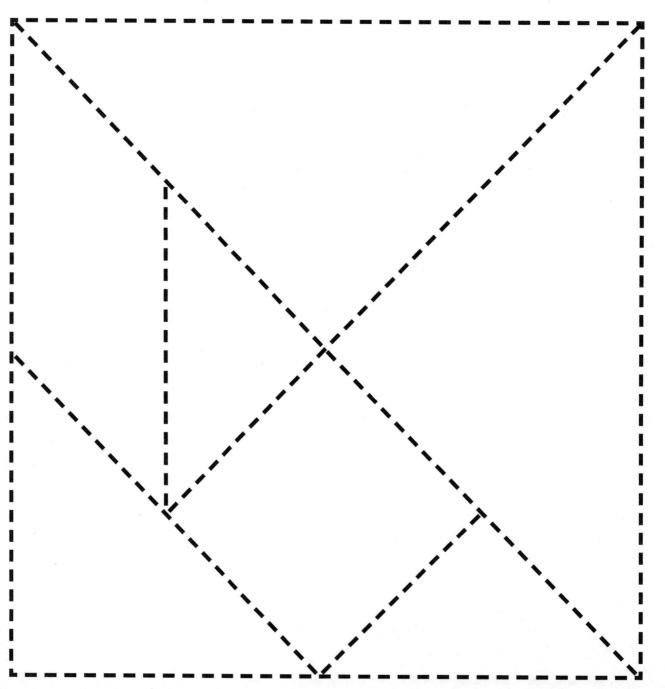

Super-Easy Shape Art Scholastic Professional Books

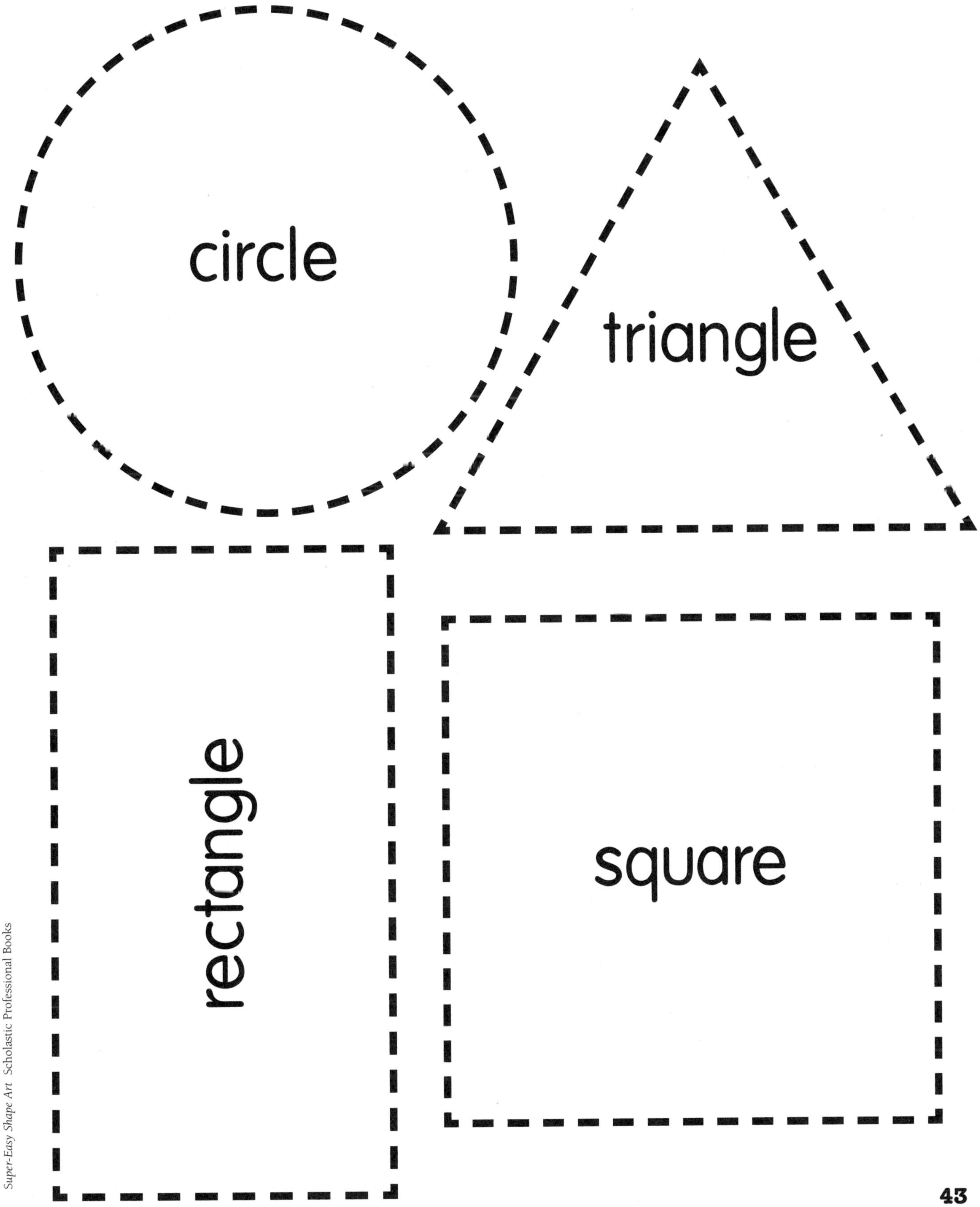

circle

triangle

rectangle

square

Super-Easy Shape Art Scholastic Professional Books

Rectangles Template

46

Mixed-Shapes Template

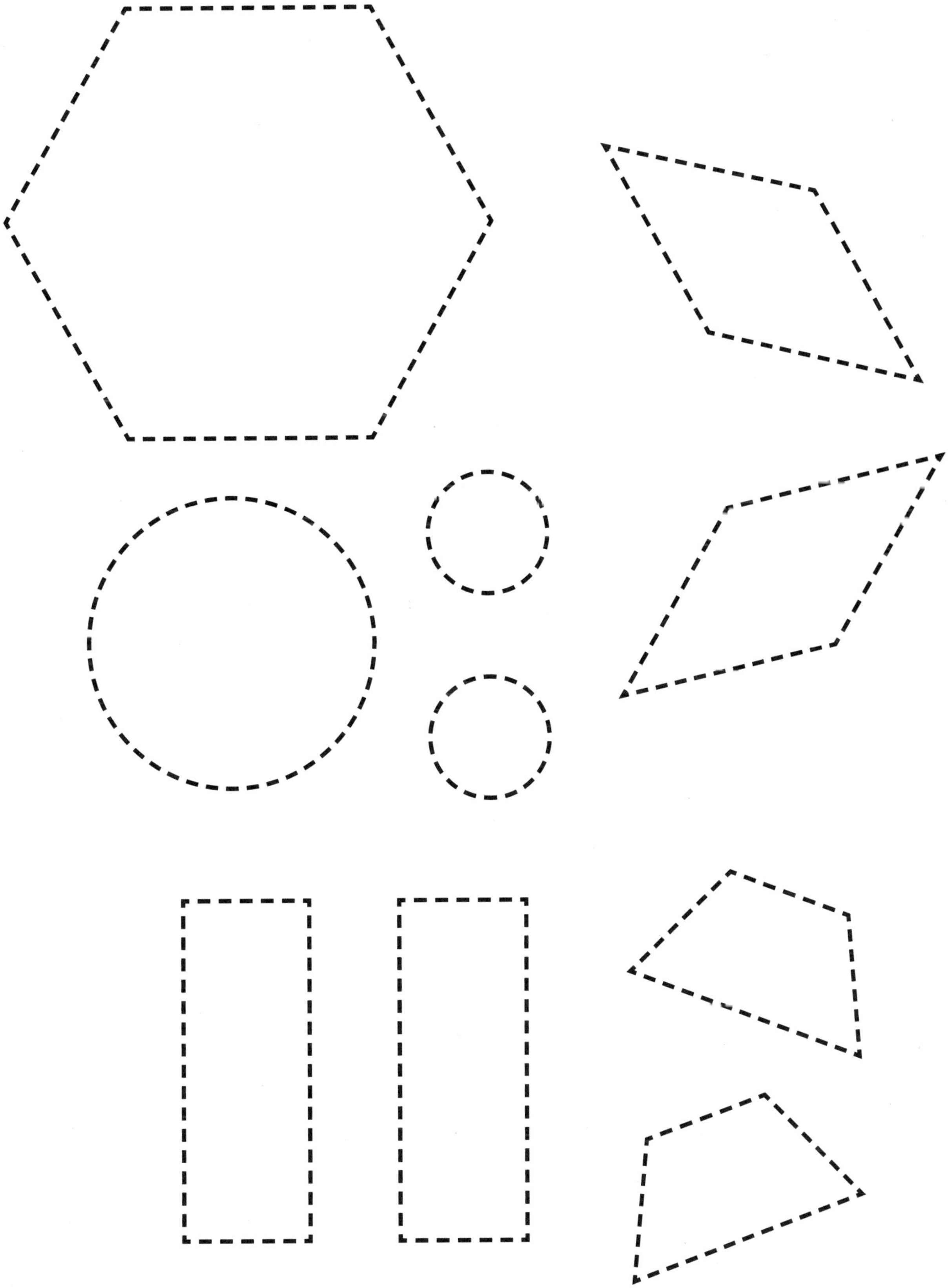

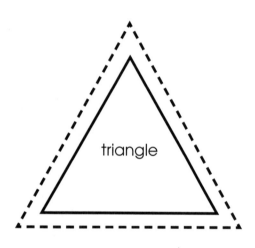

circle

square

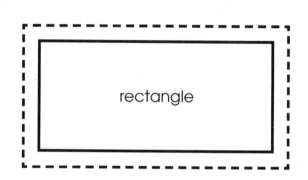

triangle

rectangle

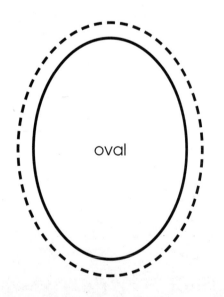

oval

rhombus

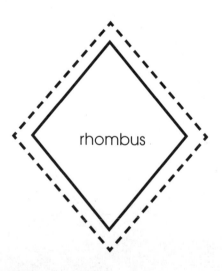

Super-Easy Shape Art Scholastic Professional Books